Focused Selling!

How To: Get What You Want Through Selling!

Focused Selling How To: Get What You Want Through Selling

Table of Contents

Focused Selling How To: Get What You Want Through
Selling

Limits of Liability/ Disclaimer of Warranty

Introduction

> ## *Our truest life is when we are in our dreams awake.*
>
> **Henry David Thoreau**

In 1986, I was a young, down and out auto salesman in my hometown of Holland Michigan. I was truly a small fish in a fairly small pond.

Frustrated and *desperate* to improve, I picked up a book by a gentleman named Zig Ziglar.

What I did next was something I had done far too little of to that point in my life… read.

My mind filled with possibilities. A fire was lit inside of me that to this day burns with greater intensity than the sun.

That book had a profound impact on my life and, although I have never met the man, I am deeply indebted to Mr. Ziglar.

My wish for you is that this book will do for you, what Mr. Ziglars' book did for me.

Focused Selling How To: Get What You Want Through Selling

Since you are reading this I *imagine* you are perhaps at a point where you want more.

More *sales*, more from *life*, **better** *health*, better *relationships*, and more *money*. Whether you are brand new to selling or a seasoned veteran, you feel a void that needs filling and here you are hoping to find some answers.

My commitment to you is simple, stick with me and I'll stick with you. Together over the next few hours or days, we'll talk about how you can get all of those outcomes you desire. Health, prosperity, love, relationships; all are yours for the taking. Stick with me, we'll discover how.

Imagine what it would be like for you to have the kind of **rewarding** sales career you're after.

How **amazing** would that feel to wake up each morning eager for the day ahead?

A day where you could make peoples' *dreams come true* and in return, yours would *too*!

And then feel the loving embrace of your family at the end of the day and know that you are truly *home*.

Come with me on this journey as together we discover how to make this the greatest year of your life and that's just the beginning.

Sound good so far?

My Mission

I love to see people "Win" in life. Nothing brings me greater joy than to see the human spirit in Victory. There are so many variables that go into success, that it becomes difficult for the individual or organization to keep track of progress, resources, strengths and weaknesses necessary to achieve it.
My mission is to bring to the individual or organization all of the "tools" and mentoring they need in order to "Win" in life. It is my pledge to never back down when everyone around you does, because that's what coaches do. A coach never accepts less of an individual or organization than they are capable of. That is the only way to ensure a "Victory" in life. That is my commitment to you, my client, my family and myself.

Tim VanRavenswaay

> *"Money's not the most important thing in life, but it does rank right up there with oxygen. I mean when you need it... you really need it!"*
>
> **Zig Ziglar**

So before we go much further, let's get acquainted, shall we?

You already know the small town Michigan boy thing, so let's fast-forward to today.

Formerly a General Manager of a Volvo dealership; now a personal coach, author, publisher, sales trainer, and certified endurance fitness trainer and an avid endurance runner.

I LOVE MY LIFE!

I love it because every day I get to help others just like you love their life too!

Over the last few years of my life, I have learned some valuable lessons about just what is really important to me. Like most salespeople I have spent a major portion of my adult life in search of the almighty dollar.

Don't get me wrong... I believe that money is awfully important. In fact, as Zig Ziglar says: "Money's not the most important thing in life, but it does rank right up there with oxygen. I mean when you need it... you really need it!" It's just not everything in life.

Focused Selling How To: Get What You Want Through Selling

What I have found ultimately to be true is; if you will make a genuine effort to have an impact or significance in others lives, the money will just be a side benefit.

In other words, when you truly go through each day with others best interests in mind, you will get far more of what you want out of life.

So here's the summary of this book. To be a true professional in the world of selling or in life for that matter, you have got to know and control what you focus on.

You've got to focus on what it is you really want it life; you've got to focus on your clients; you've got to focus on your product; you've got to focus you're marketing.

There are loads of books about closing the sale, trial closes, sales processes and selling techniques. This is not one of those books. This about you and how to get more out of your sales career and life.

This book is about paying attention to the really important stuff in each of those categories in order to keep your self on track and moving in the right direction.

How To: Get What You Want

Have you ever gone to work with a plan for the day only to reach the end of your shift and realize you accomplished nothing on the list?

Do you work from a planner with a giant To Do list?

Do you have an organized set of goals with deadlines?

Are you constantly looking for more time?

Do people around you seem to push their priorities on you with no regard for what's important to you?

Do you find yourself working harder on other peoples stuff than on what really matters to you?

What keeps you from getting what you really want out of every day?

Let me take a shot at some of your answers. I'm not a mind reader... or am I?

You find most days at work everyone wants you to work on their projects.

You probably have goals written down and you probably intend to work on them most days.

There's an odds on chance that you feel if you just had a little more time each day, uninterrupted, you could really get things crackin'.

You have a couple of projects you're working on but you really need more experience or education before you can take effective action.

And your relationships suffer because when you're at work you want to be home and vice versa.

Did I come pretty close? That's because you and I are not so different from each other.

So let me share a little secret with you.

A secret that others have paid me big money to help them understand.

And you're getting it free as part of this book.

But before I give it to you, let me ask a couple more questions. I promise I'll come back to this real quick and you'll be amazed at how simple it is!

- Do you have goals written down somewhere? Maybe just in your head right now?

- Are they truly things you can't live without?

- How did you determine your goals?

- Are you regularly attaining your goals? And setting new ones as you grow?

- How do you know when you've reached the outcome you were after?

- When you set your goals, were you conservative or wide open?

- How will you feel if you don't reach your goals?

- After you set your goals, what was the first thing you did?

- Who else knows about your goals?

- Do you have anyone besides yourself to help you stay on track?

- Do you know someone who is already getting the results you are after?

I know, I know… a lot of questions! Trust me there's plenty more where that came from.

I did not mean to confuse you or put you on the spot or frustrate you. I just wanted to help you begin to expand your thinking.

Right now, you're wondering what all this has to do with selling.

Let's look!

Ever go to work frustrated or in a bad mood?

How effective were you in that moment?

Sales can be a highly emotional career and if you carry the wrong emotions to work with you, your ability to sell will be deeply impacted.

I've seen more salespeople (myself included), who couldn't leave their baggage at the door, so to speak, and who couldn't sell their way out of a burlap sack if someone was there begging them to buy and holding their hand.

Your emotional state will affect everything you do in your sales career.

You have got to know where you stand.

Good news is you can use what I'm about to share to always be where you want to be!

"You Get What You Focus On!"

- more people than I can list here

My younger brother recently underwent knee surgery. Now you're thinking; "Oh boy! Here we go again!"

Stick with me on this one! This is where it all gets really juicy!

He is an avid runner. He's run more marathons than I have and I was always the runner in the family.

Go figure!

He has plans to begin competing in triathlons soon. And here comes this surgery.

Have you ever known anyone who had knee surgery?

What was the recovery period like?

Months, years, never quite the same?

Three weeks after having major repairs done on his knee, my brother (if you can't tell I'm pretty proud of him) did his normal Sunday morning long run of 10 miles.

Focused Selling How To: Get What You Want Through Selling

Three weeks!

It wasn't his fastest or his longest, but three weeks! WOW! Even I was impressed by my sibling rival.

Two weeks ago, one of my employees had knee surgery.

Guess how long he's out (doctor's orders)?

Two months minimum! That's if the doctor lets him come back then.

What's the difference?

Why can one person come back so quickly?

Here's the reality; my brother was very clear with his physician and the surgeon in his pre-op consultation that he needed to have minimum downtime from his training routine. The doctor responded in kind with: "We expect you to be back on the bike within 10 days."

My brother is very clear with himself about what he wants to have happen with his training and recovery.

There was no option in his mind to sit around not being active for months on end. He is very clear on his burning desire to compete in a triathlon as a master's athlete. This is not something he might want to try; it is something he is going to do!

In other words, his focus was on the outcome of getting back into training as quickly as possible and competing. He could have focused on; "Oh my gosh, I just had knee surgery!"

He could have decided he wasn't going to be training for months like most people had told him.

Instead he looked for the exceptions to the rules. Those one or two people who got extraordinary results and got right back on the horse and started riding.

He saw no possible solution but to be out running in less than a month.

In case you missed it, I've given you the secret I referred to earlier, twice already in this chapter. Here's number three:

"You get what you focus on!"

Let's move on and look at what this seemingly simple idea really means. Then we'll get in to how it applies to your selling career in the next section.

Let's go!

I asked you several times earlier if you had goals for you life, either written or at least floating around in your brain.

I then asked amongst other questions if those goals were something you simply couldn't go through life without.

Why do you think I asked that last question?

Remember when you were a kid?

Think about a time when you wanted something really bad. Maybe a new toy or to go to a friends house or anything you really, really wanted.

Remember how it consumed your attention?

Remember how creative you got at finding ways to ask for it?

Focused Selling How To: Get What You Want Through Selling

Your parents might have tried to distract you with other things or maybe just flat out said no. But you weren't interested in anything except that one thing.

What did you do?

You focused and focused and focused until you either got that outcome or you found something you wanted even more. You were young and didn't have all of the beliefs you've created over the years about what could and couldn't happen in life.

Isn't this true?

Maybe, your parents finally relented and said if you cleaned your room and did these chores, you could have it. Now if you were like most kids, you normally hated cleaning your room but what happened this time?

You sailed through your room like a professional cleaning service. You mowed the lawn like a landscaping company. The time flew by and most of it was spent not focused on the task at hand (the work) but rather on the vision of how great things would be when you had your new toy in your hands.

When it comes to training and competing, my brother has that same focus. For him it's not what he's going through in the moment (knee surgery recovery), it's what it will be like to compete in a triathlon. He envisions every inch of the race from the swim to the bike to the run. He has such a clear picture of how he will feel, what he will become, what he will experience both mentally and physically when he competes that he doesn't know anything other than to train.

This is what will get you going and keep you going.

This will move you through a day when everyone wants something from you and yet you still get the results you are after.

Focused Selling How To: Get What You Want Through Selling

What is one goal you have for yourself that you absolutely can't imagine being without?

Get a really clear vision of that outcome.

- What does it look like?

- Is it something you will have?

- Is it something you will do?

- Is it a relationship you will create or improve?

- What is it?

Write it down in the space provided below:

_____

_____

Write down all of the reasons why you absolutely can not live without this outcome:

_____

_____

_____

_____

_____

_____

Do this right now!

Don't move on without taking this crucial step to regaining control of your life.

If you can't get this working in your life, it's not going to work for you in your career.

This is not a test.

Don't worry if it's not perfect. Perfect is for machines not humans.

There are no wrong answers here because they are your personal answers.

> **If a man tries things he will certainly make many mistakes, but he will never make the greatest mistake of all... not trying!**
>
> Benjamin Franklin

Now write down all of the things you will become, have and experience as a result of this outcome. Get juicy with this stuff!

This is your life we're talking about.

Make it what you want!

Do it right now!

_____

_____

_____

_____

_____

_____

_____

Whatever the mind can conceive and believe, the mind can achieve.

Napoleon Hill

I'm Not!

Why am I making you go through this?

I'm not!

I love to help people get more out of life than they ever
imagined was humanly possible.

I love to see people expand their horizons and dream like a kid
again but you came to me.

You made a choice because you felt something had to change
and you were hoping I just might be the one to fuel that fire
inside.

Whether you're here because I hired you or I met you or you
replied to an email or one of my online advertisements or
someone referred you here, you came to me; not the other way
around… or?

Maybe meeting you was one of my goals?

Maybe my clear focused outcome was to meet you and help you
get more out of life than you ever thought possible.

Maybe when I was brainstorming like an uninhibited child, I
drew you into where you are today sharing ideas and thoughts
and proven methods for getting more out of life and out of your
selling career.

Is that possible?

Maybe you had no say in your being here at all?

© VanRavenswaay 2008

Could that be?

Wow! Those are some different ideas aren't they! The bottom-line here is you have got to expand your thinking beyond the little world that most of us live in day to day and get really creative and open to the possibilities that there is so much more than we have imagined to this point just over the horizon waiting for us.

I literally stumbled across this truth completely unintentionally on a trip back to Michigan a few years ago. And what a powerful life-changing truth it is.

I had finished a series of sales training seminars for a particular dealership and decided to take some time off to refresh and recharge. I needed the opportunity to get creative and do some serious writing. I also was looking forward to some quality time with my family whom I had not really seen much of in seven years of grinding it out in California.

I arrived in my hometown on Halloween night. My folks picked me up at the train station on a crisp October evening. The train incidentally, is a whole other story and one I'll be happy to share with anyone interested.

Very cool!

At any rate, I arrived in Michigan to temperatures in the mid-30's. Maybe not such a big deal for those of you who live in that climate, but I left my home in Southern California at about 70 degrees. And this was my first trip back to the cold in seven years.

Remember my outcomes;

1. Recharge and re-energize.
2. Get creative.
3. Do some serious writing.
4. Quality time with my family.

Focused Selling How To: Get What You Want Through Selling

These things were so deeply imbedded in my brain that this was all I could focus on.

I started getting up every morning at four-thirty to hit the road for a walk. And walk I did. Most days I would walk upwards of ten miles. I'd walk to the library to do research. I'd walk downtown to meet my folks for coffee. I'd walk to the park on the other side of town just to find some tranquility for reflection.

I was a walking fool.

My energy level soared.

About once a week I would be out somewhere with family and invariably we would run into someone who knew I was from California. The question was almost a standard;

"How you holdin' up with all this cold?"

Seems innocent enough, doesn't it? But, it really got me to thinking. I had read the statement somewhere, perhaps in a Tony Robbins book or at the library;

"You get what you focus on."

The first time those words rolled off my tongue, I don't think I even really paid attention to what I was saying. I just kind of answered the question in the moment.

The second and third time I gave that answer it started to sink in that this was really true.

I had been so focused on what I wanted to accomplish – relaxation, re-energize, creative writing, that I hadn't even realized how cold it had been. I had walked in snow storms, rain showers, cutting sub-zero temperatures that back home in California I would have avoided at all costs.

And here I was, so focused on my desired outcomes that I didn't even notice.

So now maybe when I ask if you have goals that you can't stand the thought of not achieving I'll bet you can kind of understand why. Don't panic just yet because we'll discuss this in more detail later!

But how about we get a little bit in to how to apply this to the sales profession? Come on with me!

You Get What You Focus On!

> "It isn't what you have, or who you are, or where you are, or what you are doing that makes you happy or unhappy. It is what you think about."
>
> **- Dale Carnegie**

Why do you think a book about selling would be so heavily focused on your personal development?

Think maybe your personal well being has an impact on your selling power?

Think I might be able to help you in this area?

Let's look at a typical day in the life of two salespeople and see if this whole focus thing might be making a difference in the life of both of them. One positively and one negatively.

Once we've explored it, you can decide which way you want to go.

Can you guess which way I'm betting on?

It's a typical day at ABC motors in beautiful Hometown USA. Ken and Barbie both report to work for the early shift. It's Ken's day to work the service drive so he arrives promptly at 7:30am to begin greeting customers and help the flow of traffic. It's a task he used to hate until he began to understand how valuable it is to get to know the people who already own your product.

Imagine having to show up early, greet people, show them where the customer lounge is, get them coffee and answer any questions they might have.

All of this before you are even fully awake.

Then one day it all changed for Ken. Mrs. Jones, whom he had spoken with several months prior wandered into the showroom asking for that nice young man – Ken.

It seems it was time for her to trade off her old car for a new one. Because he had taken the time to chat with her for no apparent reason while she was waiting for her car to be serviced, she trusted him.

From that day on it seemed like it just kind of snowballed.

One after another the service customers started filing in looking for that nice man – Ken.

Needless to say, he always volunteers to take over the other salespeople's shifts in the morning, in case they want to sleep in or something.

Ken is already deep in conversation when Barbie saunters through the door about an hour later. As soon as he spots Barbie, Ken separates himself from his conversation with the service customer and makes a beeline for Barbie's desk.

"Watch the floor; I'm going for some breakfast!" And out the door he goes.

Now it's all about Barbie, and not five minutes after he leaves, the first customer of the day shows up.

Focused Selling How To: Get What You Want Through Selling

Barbie is a pro! No question about it! She displays a deep seeded concern for her customers that shines like a beacon of hope in the night. Her sincerity permeates everything she does.

Within an hour or so she will have made her first sale of the day and gained another friend in the process. Someone she can actively exchange referrals with.

In the meantime, Ken returns from breakfast to realize that "Barbie got lucky" again. This is the way all of the other salespeople look at Barbie.

"She gets all of the easy customers."

You'll hear them saying this in their little huddles on the corner of the showroom.

Oh well!

Off to the service lounge to find a good magazine to read while he waits for the next customer to walk in.

No need to get to busy making phone calls yet, there's plenty of time left on this shift and besides people don't like to be bothered so early in the morning – right?

Deep into the middle of reading a great article, Ken's first customer of the day walks on to the showroom.

It's kind of an inconvenient time for Ken. The article was just getting good.

Still, he's optimistic about selling a car today so he puts down his magazine and greets the guest.

Ken brings a unique style to selling. He's decided that the best way to sell is to overwhelm his customers with product knowledge.

Focused Selling How To: Get What You Want Through Selling

He gives every customer the same full vehicle walk around no matter what their interest. Folks seem to be really impressed by his knowledge and this customer is no different.

After a wonderful presentation, the guest thanks Ken for his time and leaves.

Ken tells himself that this guy was just a tire kicker and what a waste of time that was!

Don't people understand that salespeople don't get paid unless they buy?

This seems to be happening a lot to Ken lately and it's starting to get to him.

Meanwhile, Ken watches Barbie leave for lunch with a long time friend of hers to meet a potential new customer.

Now's his chance to get a couple of deals under his belt while she's gone.

He'll get to those phone calls, just not right now.

Got to stay alert when you're the only salesperson on the showroom floor. He'll find time to follow up later or maybe tomorrow if he has to. It's just hard to find the time to get everything in.

Maybe when Barbie gets back, he can get off the floor and get organized and make some calls.

By the time Barbie returns from lunch with her new customer, picks out a car for them and does all the paperwork, Ken has already talked to 3 more guests. Maybe it's just not in the stars for him today!

That's four total presentations and not one sale. Man, I tell you what; "Sometimes you just can't catch a break!"

Focused Selling How To: Get What You Want Through Selling

Time to grab some lunch!

It's going to be a long day. This is what is referred to in the business as their "Bell to Bell" shift. That's a day when a team of salespeople work the entire day so that another team of salespeople can have a day off.

Ken kind of likes them because it means he has less competition for the day and he has more time to find his grove.

It's also the only day of the week when he leaves for lunch. Kind of his way of rewarding him self for working the long day.

Back at the dealership after a good hour and a half lunch, Ken's ready for a nap!

But now it's time to get busy! Barbie has just done her third deal of the day and his patience is starting to run a little thin.

How can she be so lucky?

What's she got going on that he doesn't?

Maybe she's getting fed deals by the manager.

There has to be something going on. They always take care of her. It's just not fair!

After about an hour of "Ken pity party of one" it's time to show what he's made of. He's going to catch up and make some deals this afternoon. No rookie sales person is going to beat him at his own game!

And here comes his first opportunity. Barbie is with a customer already and here comes a couple looking absolutely ready to buy.

And ready they are! They walk straight to the receptionist and ask for Barbie. The receptionist pages for her and soon she's standing on the showroom greeting her new guests.

She explains that she is already with a guest and asks permission to have someone else help them.

They agree and she walks them directly over to Ken, who's now looking less than enthusiastic about the prospect of having to share a commission with another salesperson, especially not Barbie. Still, a half deal is better than no deal so he reluctantly complies.

Both customers buy and now Barbie is 4 sales ahead of Ken for the day.

What on earth is she doing he wonders as he waves good-bye to the customer.

They had told him while he was getting to know them that they were given Barbie's name from a friend of a friend who had bought a car from her. They said their friend raved so highly about the experience that they couldn't resist coming down and meeting her.

With only about an hour left in the day Ken was busy reading the newspaper while Barbie sat in her office making phone calls.

He could overhear her confirming appointment times for the next couple of days. As she spoke her voice seemed to smile.

He told himself he would make his calls in the morning. Maybe he could get some of the people he'd talked to that day back in for an appointment or something. Who knows?

As the dealership lights went out the final score was;

Barbie – 4.5 sales
Ken - .5 sales

© VanRavenswaay 2008

Focused Selling How To: Get What You Want Through Selling

Barbie – 3 appointments for the next day
Ken – 0 appointments for the next day

At least tomorrow was a short day. He couldn't wait to tell the guys how lucky she was today. Everything just kind of went her way. They'd all agree with him. She's just been on a lucky streak for the last year and a half.

No matter what you sell, this is probably happening around you. Anywhere I go, I always notice there are one or two salespeople who seem to be doing most of the business.

Are they just lucky?

Are they being fed by the management?

What is it that causes this phenomenon?

Let's break it down and see what we come up with.

Tony Robbins refers to luck as Labor Under Correct Knowledge. And if you follow that definition, these individuals are definitely lucky.

Yes, these individuals really are "lucky" when day in and day out they combine what they know with some true effort.

The best of the best in sales understand that success doesn't just happen. These people know what they want and they go out and get it.

They are very clear on the results they want for their lives and they don't waste time on the distractions that come along in life.

- So what exactly does that mean for a sales person?

- What does a sales person need to be clear about in order to avoid distractions?

Focused Selling How To: Get What You Want Through Selling

- In the highly emotional business that is sales, how do the best keep it all together?

- How do the best sales people stay focused while others stray?

One of the things they all share in common is a healthy attitude. I don't mean one of those fake attitudes where everything is always roses, because it's not.

Everything in life is not always perfect, but you and only you control what things mean to you and as such you control your attitude at all times. You have to make a decision to be upset or disappointed the same as you make the decision to be happy.

Happy is not a condition, it is a choice that you and only you control if you take responsibility for your life.

When I learned this next method many years ago, it dramatically changed not only my attitude towards each day but also had a huge impact on the way others around me perceived me.

What I learned was when people ask you how you are doing, you always tell them you are: "Excellent" or "Outstanding" or "Fantastic", but you'll get better!

Now I know you may be thinking: "This guy's nuts!" Am I always fantastic?

Well of course not, but the people I come in contact with don't know that. They only know what I tell them and when I say I'm "Outstanding", I have now set a standard for myself that I have to live up to.

The truth is, if you say it often enough you can't help but start to smile and suddenly your attitude does take a turn for the better.

Is everything always perfect in my world? Not by a long stretch.

Focused Selling How To: Get What You Want Through Selling

I am a human being just like every body else. I have ups and downs. I have good days and bad, but when I set a high standard for myself I can't help but keep looking up and reaching for it.

I have also come to understand over the years that no matter how bad you think things may be, you don't have to look very far to find someone who is far worse off than you.

Many times when I tell somebody I am excellent they will say something like: "Well what are you so happy about?" My standard reply is: "Any day that I wake up and don't read my name in the obituaries is a pretty good day to me!" And of course at that point they start to laugh and say well that's ridiculous you couldn't possibly read your name in the… and my point is made.

The fact that I am a healthy, living, breathing human being, who is able to get up and go after life in whatever manner I choose, makes me pretty outstanding every day!

Another interesting thing happens when I take this approach to each day. Misery loves company.

Zig Ziglar says: "One of the downsides to throwing a 'pity-party' is that very few people attend, and nobody ever brings any gifts!"

A lot of the time when someone asks you how you are doing; what are they thinking? They don't want to hear how you're doing… they just want you to ask them so they can bring you into their "pity-party".

When you fire off: "I'm outstanding, but I'll get better!" it stops them dead in their tracks. They start thinking things like:"Well, I'm not going to get any sympathy here, I need to go find somebody else to join my party." Net result… not only do you put yourself in the right frame of mind, but you also dodge another bad attitude bullet

Focused Selling How To: Get What You Want Through Selling

How do I know this works?

I know from personal first-hand experience.

I will warn you of something that's going to happen. If you have been a negative person whether first-hand or just guilty by association, when you first start saying things like: "Fantastic" or "Outstanding", people are going to look at you kind of funny. They're probably going to want to take your temperature and maybe send you to the doctor to see if you've got some kind of virus or something.

Don't let them derail you! When they ask you what's gotten into you, why not answer them with the truth?

I have decided that I want to get the most out of life that I can each and every day! I know that I cannot possibly do that if I am spending all of my time whining and complaining about every single little thing that happens.

The saying goes: "Don't sweat the small stuff… and everything is small stuff!"

Am I always excellent? No, but I will get better each and every minute of each and every day if I choose to!

The next thing you need to look at if you want to get and maintain the right attitude is your relationships or the people you associate with.

If you want to be successful in selling, I mean build a professional career for the long haul; you have to surround yourself with the right kind of people.

You are in a profession that requires a high level of integrity if you want to make a career out of it. Most of us have met what I call the "60-day wonders". They come into a business; sell a bunch of product by deceiving, manipulating and outright lying to customers and in many cases the business owner. After about

60 days they have to move on to another store because all of their lies start to catch up with them. Usually, some sales manager is left cleaning up their mess for the next 60 days.

If you want to build a true career where you stay in the same place, have a clientele, get referrals and earn a decent living, you have got to have integrity.

If you are really putting forward the effort to be the right kind of person at work and you are going home to a different type of environment there is no way you're going to make it.

What do I mean?

I mean if the main influences in your life outside of work are negative or deceitful people or individuals who drink too much or maybe even do drugs, how can you possibly expect to maintain a good attitude and integrity.

Unfortunately, most people tend to follow the lead of their peers. Particularly if you are just starting to understand the value of having the right attitude, you will be very susceptible to the negative influences of those around you. If you have just gone along for the ride most of your life, when you start to work on the positive your friends and those around you may ridicule or tease you. They may not even intend to make you feel awkward, but they won't understand. If they are true friends, they will accept you for who you are trying to be. If they don't, you need to decide if that is really a friend or not. True friends always want the best for you.

You may be amazed to find how much better your relationships are when you share them with those who support your efforts instead of try to break you down.

Sometimes the hardest thing we face as we try to improve ourselves is the reality that some of the people we have allowed to be in our lives don't really belong there. I can tell you from personal experience that you cannot get and maintain the right attitude if you are surrounded with the wrong kind of people.

It's your life… you decide!

Still another area you need to be certain about is your chosen profession. Many times when I have met people for the first time the conversation comes around to what I do for a living.

Invariably, when I tell people that I am a salesperson or a sales trainer, someone in the crowd will come back with: "Oh great! A salesman. Even worse, a car salesman!"

Obviously, there are some people in our business who have brought that stigmatism upon the rest of us. However if you are truly in this business as your chosen profession and you demonstrate integrity in your actions every day, these kinds of statements can be highly insulting and somewhat demoralizing.

You need to personally believe in the profession you are in and understand that many people who demean or look down on salespeople don't really understand how our economy works.

Many people don't understand that without salespeople selling, they very likely would not have a job to go to each day. To understand this concept completely read the verse that follows entitled: "I Am a Salesperson"

I Am A Salesperson!
Author Unknown

I am proud to be a salesperson because more than any other person I, and millions of others like me, built America. The person who builds a better mousetrap… or a better anything… would starve to death if they waited for people to beat a pathway to their door. Regardless of how good, or how needed, the product or service might be, it has to be sold.

Focused Selling How To: Get What You Want Through Selling

Eli Whitney was laughed at when he showed his cotton gin. Edison had to install his electric light free of charge in an office building before anyone would even look at it. The first sewing machine was smashed to pieces by a Boston mob. People scoffed at the idea of railroads. They thought that even traveling thirty miles an hour would stop the circulation of the blood! McCormick strived for fourteen years to get people to use his reaper. Westinghouse was considered a fool for stating that he could stop a train with wind. Morse had to plead before ten Congresses before they would even look at his telegraph. The public won't go around demanding these things; they had to be sold!

They needed thousands of salespeople, trailblazers, pioneers, people who could persuade with the same effectiveness as the inventor could invent. Salespeople took these inventions, sold the public on what these products could do, and taught businessmen how to make a profit from them.

As a salesperson I've done more to make America what it is today than any other person you know. I was just as vital in your great-great-grandfather's day as I am in yours, and I'll be just as vital in your great-great-grandson's day. I have educated more people; created more jobs; taken more drudgery from the laborer's work; given more profits to businessmen; and have given more people a fuller and richer life than anyone in history. I've dragged prices down, pushed quality up, and made it possible for you to enjoy the comforts and luxuries of automobiles, radios, electric refrigerators, televisions, and air-conditioned homes and buildings. I've healed the sick, given security to the aged, and put thousands of young men and women through college. I've made it possible for inventors to invent, for factories to hum, and for ships to sail the seven seas.

How much money you find in your paycheck next week, and whether in the future you will enjoy the luxuries of prefabricated homes, stratospheric flying planes, and a new world of jet propulsion and atomic power depends on me. The loaf of bread that you bought today was on a baker's shelf because I made sure that a farmer's wheat got to a mill, that the mill made the wheat into flour, and that the flour was delivered to your baker.

Focused Selling How To: Get What You Want Through Selling

Without me the wheels of industry would come to a grinding halt. And with that, jobs, marriages, politics, and freedom of thought would be a thing of the past. I AM A SALESPERSON and I am both proud and grateful that as such I serve my family, my fellow man, and my country!

What a powerful and true statement about our profession. You should be proud that as a salesperson you could impact the lives of so many people just by being a true professional.

There are many other things you can do to get and maintain the right attitude. Incidentally, your attitude is so important and is affected by so many different things that it is actually the subject of a completely separate training program. Hopefully, you will get the jest of what I am trying to share with you here and it will peak your interest to explore it at greater length on your own.

One more quick tip:

Join what Zig Ziglar refers to as "Automobile University". Most of us particularly here in Southern California spend a great deal of time in our automobiles. Most of us also have either a cassette or CD player in our cars. I would encourage you to use that drive time to listen to motivational or educational material.

At the back of this book is a list of some suggested reading materials, many of those books are also available in audio form.

I believe it was one of the major universities in our country who completed a study which showed that if you live in a major metropolitan area and drive an average of 12000 miles per year; in three years of driving and listening you can acquire the equivalency of a two year college education. "Automobile University" Sign up today!

Focused Selling How To: Get What You Want Through Selling

Remember that getting and keeping the right attitude takes daily effort and attention. Keep at it and you will definitely be on the road to true success in selling!

That being said, attitude is not the only thing that the top sales people have in common. As I started to allude to earlier, they all are very clear on what they are after in life.

If you come to work each day with no expectations as to what you are after, guess what you'll get?

You'll get exactly whatever the world decides to send your way. With no true results to focus on, you are going to fall victim to whatever anyone else wants to happen.

When you don't have a purpose and a plan, you are going to go through each day like tumbleweed in the wind.

If you want results, know what you want! I'll repeat that one more time; if you want results, know what you want!

Just saying I'd like to sell a car today doesn't make for a very certain outcome.

To start with, I'd never say I'd like to, because it's just a weak statement right from the start.

I would change that to I'm going to sell a car today.

All I changed was "like to" to "going to", but it makes a huge impact on your mindset.

Changing a couple of words makes a difference, but it's not the answer we're looking for here.

Remember, L.U.C.K.?

Labor under correct knowledge means that you fully understand what it takes to succeed in your chosen profession. In this case that means sales. The best of the best understand that it's not simply enough to have a great attitude (although it does help). You have got to know and acquire the skill sets that are required in the profession you are in.

If you are a sales person, you have to understand how to get to know your customers.

- How to build rapport.

- How to determine your customer needs.

- How to build a lasting relationship with your customer.

- How to find more customers when they aren't breaking down the doors to get to you.

- How to keep the main thing the main thing.

- How to turn your satisfied customers into your best resource for new customers.

- How to build real trust with your customers.

Then on top of all of this, you have got to get very clear on why it is that you do what you do.

Most of us have other reasons for doing what we do in life.

In other words, you probably aren't selling whatever you're selling just to sell.

You are counting on getting a commission for selling your product. And that's still not the reason you sell.

Now you might be thinking I'm a little nuts (and I am), but bare with me on this.

Focused Selling How To: Get What You Want Through Selling

What ultimately do you want when you sell a car and earn a commission?

To pay your bills?

And what would that give you?

Transportation and housing and food.

And what would that give you?

Peace of mind, a great family relationship, security, etc.

And what would that give you?

Happiness.

When it all comes down to it, most of us just want to be happy. The amazing thing is that we don't need to do any of these things to be happy. As I said earlier, you can be happy anytime you decide to.

The sooner you understand that the sooner you can release it to reality.

If you can focus on what you will get when you sell a car or whatever your product is, it will be much easier to keep yourself on track doing what you need to do.

It will motivate you to stay up late or get up early, just to get the extra knowledge you need to be better than everyone around you.

Maybe the business you're in is not your ultimate dream career. Perhaps it is simply a means to an end. If you don't want it to become your life's mission, you better find a way to be really good at it really fast or you may never get out.

Focused Selling How To: Get What You Want Through Selling

That's a sad truth that far too many people know. They started in a job just to make some money, thinking they would break through and get out after a short period of time and twenty years later, they're still in the same old job, about as miserable as a human being can be.

That's kind of where Ken from our story is. He knows what he would like to do, but he's never really committed to doing what it takes to get the results he's after.

I'm not a hundred percent convinced that he even knows why he's in the business of selling. If he doesn't figure it out soon, he'll end up stocking shelves at the local grocery store because he'll lose the job he has right now.

As it sits right now, he spends way too much time being distracted by everything and anything, regardless of the importance.

He has no target to aim for!

There! I said it! How can you possibly stay focused on where you're going if you don't even know where it is you're going?

And listen up, because this little truth applies just as much if not more to your personal life as it does to selling.

Remember earlier when I asked about the things in life that you wanted that you couldn't stand the thought of not having?

How do you focus on something like that?

Just like the example of when you were a kid. When you are clear about what you want, you will do whatever it takes to get to it. People will go to the ends of the earth in a quest to have something they really truly desire.

That's what great sales people do.

Focused Selling How To: Get What You Want Through Selling

They are completely clear on what they want and the commitment it takes to get there.

I did not say, they always know exactly how to get there at first, but they are clear on what they want. And they are clear that they will do what it takes to get there.

So let's look at Barbie from our little dealership story.

She obviously has a clear vision of what she wants. When she gets to work, she begins doing exactly what it takes to accomplish it.

She has obviously acquired the skills she needs to be effective at her job.

And at the end of the day when it would be easy to rest on her laurels and just relax, she's busy setting up her plan for tomorrow, making all of the necessary calls to fill her appointment calendar.

That my friend is a pro!

Ken may, for all intents be a much smoother talker, but he lacks a clear direction and so each day he flounders through his shifts miserably.

The sales person who is clearly focused on the results they are after, whatever they may be will always be the "lucky" one in the crowd.

And that's lucky by design.

The Initial Contact

When you have company over to your house or if you have someone you know come and visit you at the office, how do you greet them?

Do you welcome them?

Shake their hands?

Offer them a beverage?

Offer them a place to sit?

Maybe take them on a tour of the place if they've never been there before?

Why would you do any differently to the prospect that walks in the door that you don't know?

Aren't they welcome?

Didn't your business owner probably spend thousands… maybe hundreds of thousands of dollars trying to get them to come in?

We've already discussed your attitude and so I know that it won't be the reason you are less than hospitable and professional with a prospect.

Why is it that we don't welcome every guest to our business with open arms?

Maybe it's because we don't fully appreciate their value to us as salespeople… even if they don't buy.

Focused Selling How To: Get What You Want Through Selling

You may have seen this worksheet or a variation of it at some point in the past. Incidentally, it works for any sales business, not just for automobiles. Let's look at an example.

I will precaution you to be honest with yourself.

If you talk to 2 prospects on average per day... don't try to fudge the numbers and say you only talk to 1.

Doing that will not help anyone, not on this worksheet or anywhere else in your sales career.

Prospects per day   ____

X

Days Worked per Month   ____

equals

Prospects per Month   ____

Sales per month   ____

X

Average Commission   ____

equals

© VanRavenswaay 2008

Average Income per Month   _____

Average Income per Month   _____

divided by

Prospects per Month   _____

Value per Prospect   _____

Imagine every person that walks through the doors

hands you $_____. Whether they buy or not!

Let's say you talk to 2 prospects per day and you work an average of 25 days per month. We fill those numbers in on the worksheet. Using those numbers we arrive at the fact that you talk to 50 people a month about purchasing your products. Write that down.

Now let's look at your income. Let's say that you are selling an average of 10 widgets per month and your average commission per sale is $300.00. Write that down. 10 widgets times $300.00 per sale equals $3000.00. This is not rocket science!

The last section shows you the value of every person you talk to, whether you sell them a vehicle or not.

Quite simply, $3000.00 divided by 50 prospects equals $60.00 per person.

Why do I do this illustration? It's kind of like the old fear of speaking tool, where they tell you if you have to stand up in front of a group of people and you're terrified by the prospect of doing so… just picture them all in their underwear and you won't be able to help but start laughing. When you start laughing you relax and can go on with your speech or presentation.

If you will imagine that every person you talk to walks up and hands you $60.00, whether you sell them a thing or not, you start to appreciate their value.

What would happen if you learned and I mean really studied and learned the techniques we discuss here and were able to significantly increase that $60.00 to let's say $100.00?

Then you were also able to use your skills to increase the number of sales you made out of the people you spoke with.

What would that do to your income?

What would that do to your approach to each and every person who walked into your business each day?

My whole point here is that no matter what your mood is or what time it is, each person you speak with represents an income opportunity for you and deserves to be treated accordingly.

So, how do you do that?

Over the years I have seen and heard a large handful of different speakers try to come up with different ways to approach a customer. I have heard people say the old way is too corny or canned. The buyer of today is more sophisticated and you can't treat them the same or speak to them the same as we used to. To all of that I say… HUH??????????

I am going to tell you that the way we have been greeting people for years is still the best way to do it. A lot of people have tried, with a tremendous amount of effort to revolutionize the sales profession and yet, here we are today with perhaps a few additional tools, such as the internet, but the exact same customers.

Don't get me wrong… I think that internet departments and call centers and those types of additions to a business are essential to keeping up with the way that people communicate today, but if the people who staff those departments don't utilize and understand the basic principals of selling, the results for the business will be no different than if they did not have those departments at all.

When you approach a customer the conversation is just this simple:

Good Morning/Afternoon/Evening! Welcome to Your Business Name!

My name is Your Name, and you are?

This is not rocket science. I didn't just make this up and in fact if you asked any sales trainer with a half-grain of integrity, where that opening line came from, they would tell you they did not know… it has just always been the greeting.

Why is this line so effective?

Incidentally, in about 90 percent of the cases where you say these words, you will get a positive response and a name from the prospect. For now don't worry about the other 10 percent, but we will talk about them a little later. I believe that a large part of why this works goes back to what I was saying earlier.

Focused Selling How To: Get What You Want Through Selling

Why do you welcome guests to your house?

You greet them enthusiastically because you invited them and you want them to enjoy themselves while they are visiting.

Isn't that the truth?

Isn't that the way you want guests of your business to feel?

Let's look at it a little deeper. Now, I could just say to you if I was your boss… do it because I said so, but I have learned as I said earlier that if you really understand the "why", you are much more likely to buy in to what I am selling and that is exactly what I am here for!

Let's use car buying for a minute as an example.

Buying an automobile is something the average consumer does somewhere around every 3 ½ to 4 years. Now with a few exceptions, most salespeople have not been at their current dealership for that long. That means that the prospect considering another Volvo probably does not know anyone at the dealership, with the possible exception of a service person.

That, by the way is a relationship we will talk about later which can be crucial to your sales success and we will discuss it a greater length when we talk about building your success machine.

My point is, they are coming in "Cold".

Who would you rather buy your next computer or big screen TV or car from?

Someone you know or a complete stranger with whom you have no relationship?

Do you think a consumer who walks in the door at the dealership or your business feels any differently?

Of course not!

We all have different ways of greeting our friends, depending on our personalities. On any given day if you pay enough attention you can probably hear a hundred different greetings.

We hear things like:

"What's up?"

"What's happening?"

"How's it going?"

"How are you today?"

"How's your day so far?"

"How do you do?"

"How You Doin'?"

The list goes on and on. You can get away with saying a lot of different things to people you know, because you know them. The reality is, you can't do that with a perfect stranger and get consistent results.

Let's say a man comes into a dealership because his wife has been nagging him about replacing the family minivan with a new station wagon. He has found an hour between sales calls to do some researching so he stops in.

Every customer he has called on has rejected him.

Dutifully he stops in to find the right vehicle for his wife. His day to this point has been miserable.

The first words out of your mouth are: "How's your day?"

Focused Selling How To: Get What You Want Through Selling

He may not, in fact, probably won't, tell you about his day, but throughout the rest of his visit with you that is all he will think about.

Net result… anything you say will likely fall on deaf ears and as helpful as you may think you have been to him; there is a good chance he will end up somewhere else, telling everyone he knows how poor the service was over at your store.

A little extreme?

Trust me when I say it happens everyday at dealerships and other businesses all around the country.

Selling is a very emotional business. As a salesperson you need to learn when to bring out the emotions of a customer and when to leave them alone.

The best positively emotional thing you can do at the moment of initial contact with a prospect is give them a professional warm and positive welcome as in the example.

Let's look for a moment at the other thing that is happening in this simple greeting:

… And your name is?

Why is this little portion of the greeting so important to you and the prospect throughout the entire sales process?

Well, there are actually two reasons.

First of all, people like to hear their name. I didn't make this up. Studies have shown that the repetition of a persons' name throughout a conversation draws them into it.

Second, during every initial contact between two people control of the conversation is established. Although it is important to allow the prospect to feel they have control, if you want to sell more and help more people, you have got to have control of the sales process right from the beginning.

The best and really the only consistent way to gain control is by asking questions and get the prospects talking. When I say get them talking... I mean about what you want them to talk about. The first thing you want them talking about is their name!

Let me ask you a question.

How many of you are currently greeting your customers this way?

How hard will it be for you to do this on a daily customer-by-customer basis?

If you are not doing this... why not?

Everything we talk about throughout this book will take some practice to perform, but if you truly want to be a professional in the world of selling... it is absolutely something you need to do.

I want each of you to stand up right now, go to the mirror and practice your greeting.

Remember to smile when you greet them because as we already discussed, whether you sell them anything or not they are paying you.

Did you fumble with the words? Don't worry, just keep practicing and you'll get it.

Can you see how using a warm professional greeting will be of benefit to you?

Can you see how it makes sense for you to get and use the prospects name right from the start?

Focused Selling How To: Get What You Want Through Selling

Can you see how asking questions, besides giving you important information, will also allow you to guide the prospect through the process?

Before we move on, I would like to briefly discuss the difference between selling and persuading and just how significant this difference is to you in your sales career.

What Is Selling?

Do you believe that selling is something that you do to the prospect or something you do for the prospect?

One of the most difficult things new salespeople struggle with results from a misunderstanding of what selling is really all about. When you're new in the business of selling, you'll hear things like: "Take Control" and immediately panic, because you don't like the idea of being controlled and you're maybe uncomfortable with the idea of doing that to someone else.

You start to picture the last time you went out to buy something, and you had some "slimy" salesperson breathing down your neck, trying to push you in to something you didn't even want.

Maybe you did want it, you just didn't want to be pushed or controlled.

This brings up a conversation, which we will get into in greater detail later about word selections.

Many times when I am speaking I will use certain words because of their perceived value or meaning. In other words, the majority of people think of the exact same thing when I say them.

Spend time with me and you will hear me repeat over and over again that you have got to ask lots and lots of questions. I stated earlier that one of the reasons we ask questions is to gain control.

Focused Selling How To: Get What You Want Through Selling

There is that word again.

In a recent training session I had a young man that was having an extremely difficult time with that word. We decided that the better choice of words would be "Guide".

In other words, if we don't ask questions, we won't be able to guide the prospect through the sales process.

For the moment let's forget about the word "Control" and focus on just why it is that you need to "Guide" the prospect through the sales process and just what that really means.

Incidentally, if you're not in sales and you're reading this don't pretend to be shocked that I would suggest that a salesperson take control of the sales process.

Salespeople have an obligation to guide you through a process that you may know little or nothing about in order to ultimately help you get what's best for you and we'll talk about that a little more in a bit.

Unless you are brand new to the world of selling, you have probably gone through a situation with a prospect where you sold them on your product. I mean you really sold them on the product. They were in complete agreement that:

Yes, it is a great product;

Yes, it did meet their needs and wants:

Yes, they could afford it, and still they did not buy.

This can be an extremely frustrating situation. So, why did it happen?

Let me ask you this: How many of you have sold a product to someone who is still enjoying the benefits of using it today?

© VanRavenswaay 2008

How many of you earned a commission when you sold that product?

How many of you still have all of the commission you earned from that sale?

How many of you have a majority of your customers enjoying their products long after you've spent the commissions?

Now unless you're selling a slip-shod product, which I hope you're not, it is reasonable to say that your customers are almost all enjoying the products you sold them for a long time. And I can say that in most cases, you as a salesperson have spent that commission or part of it shortly after the sale (If not before it).

Am I right?

How many of you believe that you represent an O.K. product? A good product? A Great product?

How many of you believe that assuming the prospect can buy... there is something for pretty much everyone who walks into your place of business? When I say everyone who walks in to your business, it's because most people coming in aren't there to buy your competitors products.

O.K., so we know that you sell a pretty good product. It offers something for most everyone who walks in that can buy.

We also know that in probably 99.9% of the cases, the customers are enjoying the benefits of your products' ownership long after the salesperson's commission is spent

Who gets the better side of a sales transaction?

Is it the salesperson or the customer?

Focused Selling How To: Get What You Want Through Selling

Let me ask you another question. If you're a Volvo salesperson and your customer were comparing your S40 to a Toyota Camry, which car would they be better off in if they had an accident?

Over my few years selling Volvos, I would have to say that at least once a month I heard of a life that was saved because of driving a Volvo.

How do you think those Volvo owners feel about the salesperson that convinced them to buy one?

And what if you really sold someone on the Volvo, I mean they completely agreed that it was a great vehicle, but they didn't buy. Instead of the Volvo he goes out and buys the Brand X. The next day his wife is driving the new car and is hit head on and killed. At the scene of the accident, the emergency services people tell him the only kind of car they've ever seen survive that kind of impact is a Volvo.

Who's he upset with?

Isn't it the salesperson that didn't care enough to take the time to persuade him to get the Volvo?

You bet it is!

Now maybe and I mean just maybe... this is an over dramatization, but not by much and it does make this point:

You represent an outstanding product, whatever the brand. I've given you a couple of very valid reasons why you can and should make every effort to persuade them to invest in your product.

First, we know that with very rare exceptions, your customers are enjoying the use of their purchases long after you've spent your commissions, which means they are definitely the winners in the sales transaction.

© VanRavenswaay 2008

Second, we know that, in the case of Volvos as an example, they save lives. I am not the exception to the rule. There are literally thousands of people who because of their association with Volvo over the years have heard similar "life-saving" stories.

Let me ask you this question again: Is selling something you do to the prospect or something you do for the prospect?

When you take steps to effectively persuade a prospect to make a decision that is in his or her best interest, selling is something you do for the customer.

So how about the guy we talked about earlier.

The one you really, really sold?

He agreed with every word you said, except he still didn't buy.

How come? I mean... why not?

Over the last few minutes I have used the word "persuade" several times. I substituted it in places where if it weren't me talking, others might have used the word "sell". I believe there is a substantial difference between the two words and understanding that difference can make a significant change in your career.

What sells?

Doesn't advertising sell?

Look at McDonalds' advertising.

Doesn't it sell?

Boy I will tell you I love a fresh Quarter-Pounder with Cheese (Although these days they're not in my diet)! When I see their commercials, my mouth starts to water just thinking about one.

© VanRavenswaay 2008

How about Nike's commercials?

Don't they sell?

When you see a commercial for some of their shoes on a professional athlete, don't you buy into their product?

How about BMW?

When you see a BMW commercial with one of their automobiles driving with exhilaration down a winding road... don't you buy into the fact that you should have one?

Selling in essence is creating a need where it did not exist. Now, don't get me wrong, I believe that the type of selling we are talking about here is essential to your success as a salesperson. If manufacturers and dealers didn't "Sell" their products, people would not be coming in to see your products.

Let me share a quick story about me with you to help illustrate my next point.

For probably the last 10 years of my life, I was as Zig Ziglar would say; decidedly overweight. When I say decidedly, I mean: I decided to eat too much and I decided not to exercise consistently and I decided not to eat the right foods.

My younger brother (One year younger) eats a very well maintained and structured diet. He also makes a commitment to do both cardio and strength training. He is in probably the best shape and condition of his adult life.

When we talk about eating and diet, I trust what he says because he is a living example of what he says.

He has persuaded me that it is in my best interest (I just said the key ingredient... my best interest) to have a better more consistent diet.

Focused Selling How To: Get What You Want Through Selling

When I am holding training sessions my diet suffers. I will eat a light breakfast before leaving the house, but I will not eat any lunch.

Instead I prefer to take a short walk around the neighborhood of the dealership where I'm training if conditions permit. I have found that if I eat lunch I tend to be sluggish in the afternoon sessions, but if I just go for a walk I have a chance to reflect on the morning and prepare for the afternoon.

Consequently, when it comes to the end of the day it would be very easy to swing into one of those freeway close establishments... like McDonalds' and grab a quick meal.

I don't do it.

Don't get me wrong, I am not down on McDonalds' or any of the other fast food restaurants at our disposal today and having been in this business for so many years I know how convenience usually takes precedence over true nutritional quality.

It's just that my brother has persuaded me to take better care of my diet and although he doesn't condone my not eating during the day, he absolutely doesn't recommend McDonalds' either.

What's the difference between McDonalds' and my brother?

McDonalds' does a great job of selling me on its products and its convenience, but my brother knows me and I know that when he persuades me to do something it is because he has my best interests in mind.

Do you think that honestly speaking, McDonalds' cares one bit about my health?

Absolutely not!

They care about getting me to come in and spend my money.

Focused Selling How To: Get What You Want Through Selling

Did they ever tell me in all of those years of my overeating that I should have the small size portions instead of the super-size?

Of course not, in fact they suggested super-sizing didn't they?

Of course they do offer diet drinks and salads.

I'm not picking on them; I'm actually pointing out what a fantastic job they do of selling.

Can you see the difference between selling and persuading?

Here are my humble definitions of the two words:

Selling – creating a want or need where it did not exist.

Persuading - convincing another to take action based on something they already know is in their best interest.

When you understand the difference and start focusing on what is in your prospects best interest, you will be able to persuade more of those people who were "sold", to take action.

In our example earlier, we said you really sold the fellow on the vehicle, but what you did not do was persuade him that it was in his best interest to take action right then and there.

Learning to persuade someone starts with getting to know your prospect and as the next chapter indicates… It's not all about You!

It's Not All About You!

To start this section out I'd like to share an article with you that I wrote a few years ago for my newsletter.

I Heard Every Word You Said... I Just Wasn't Listening!

Guilty as charged! Most of us are! It happens not just in the sales business, but also in our everyday lives as well. Someone asks a question or makes a statement to you and you thought you were listening. You heard every word they said, however you have absolutely no idea what they are talking about. Unfortunately, it's not because you don't understand what they are saying... it's just that you aren't paying attention.

Do this to a friend... they'll be upset. Do this to a customer... you stand a pretty good chance of losing a sale. The real problem for the customer in most cases is not that they think you are rude. It's actually the fact that the customer is probably telling you how and what to sell them, but you're not paying attention.

Some folks might think that this is a common rookie mistake, and it is, however it is also just as predominant with seasoned pros. In fact, it is probably more likely to occur once you get comfortable with your position in a dealership. When you're new, you pay extra attention to everything for fear of missing something very important. Once you get comfortable the tendency is to think you know everything... including what the customer needs without them telling you.

Don't believe me? Here's an example:

A 55-year-old man walks into the dealership and says he wants to look at the new "X-Model" sedan because he has heard it's very sporty and it is time for him to get something a little more fun to drive. Being the consummate professional that you think you are, you lead him directly across the lot to where this vehicle is located. On your way you pass a great looking coupe. It's your best performing and selling sports car.

© VanRavenswaay 2008

Focused Selling How To: Get What You Want Through Selling

He pauses and asks a couple of quick questions about it and comments on how sexy it looks. You answer his questions in rapid-fire manner and then drag him over to the car he told you he was looking for. You spend a fair amount of time presenting the vehicle to him, even taking a demonstration drive in his favorite color. Being the pro that you are, you have selected a vehicle that seems to match every option and color combination he wants. A half an hour later you are standing around with the other salespeople telling them what a jerk that guy was. He made you go for a drive and everything and then just said thanks and left. Can you believe that? The nerve of that guy! Doesn't he know you get paid to sell cars not go on demo drives?

So what happened? Was this guy really out just to kill some time? There is always that chance, but in most cases that is not what was going on at all. To find the answer you need to understand what listening is really all about. Some people believe that listening is just hearing the words coming out of someone's mouth. In some very rare cases, the spoken words are the only communication being given and they mean exactly what is said. I stress... in very rare cases. Human beings communicate with several different senses. I know I'm probably not the first person to tell you about body language, voice inflection and those types of things. The reality is all of these things come into play when listening. Those things aside... particularly in the United States, we have a language which can have multiple meanings or interpretations. A lot of us also have a tendency not to say exactly what we mean. We may say what is most practical or seems like the most logical or responsible thing, however that is the farthest thing from what we really want. In our example the customer needed or felt the practical car to look at was the sedan. What do you think would have happened if the salesperson had listened to what the customer's hidden signals were saying and spent more time exploring the sport coupe? I have seen it time and time again where some one comes in saying one thing and leaves with what logically would be the farthest from what they said. Why? Probably because a salesperson was paying attention enough to realize that what the customer really wanted was something totally different.

What we need to do as salespeople is spend more time paying attention to what the customer is really saying. Most people will not give you their buying motivation without you asking a lot of questions. Back to our example again, the customer gave off some pretty clear signals that he was not saying what he meant. What if the salesperson had asked some simple questions like; "How are you going to be using the new car?" or "Do you normally carry passengers or is this more of a personal vehicle?" or "What's the occasion?" There is a wealth of good questions that could have been asked that would have probably revealed this customer's buying motives. I'm sure that most of us would have loved to be the salesperson with this type of customer. I'm also certain that most of us have had this same customer and unfortunately done the same sort of thing as the salesperson in the example.

There are a couple key things you can do to avoid being this salesperson. When listening to someone speaking make a conscious effort to focus on what they are saying. A very high percentage of people are thinking about what they are going to say next when someone else is speaking. A good method for making certain you are paying attention is to rephrase what the other person is saying in the form of a question or statement. Not only will you be certain of what was said but also the other person will be sure that you heard them correctly. An example of this is; "I'm looking for a vehicle with good performance." You might say; "So performance is important in your next vehicle?" and you might follow up with; "Tell me what performance means to you." The person I am speaking with knows I paid attention and my follow up question opens them up to disclose more information about what they are really interested in. Whenever I feel like I am not communicating well with other people, I will make an effort to review the conversations I have with them. How many times was I thinking about what I would say next or possibly not even thinking about the conversation at all? This is a quick way to get back on track. It's almost scary how many times we really aren't mentally involved in conversations we have. I'm sure you've had it happen to you and sometimes you may not even realize that the other person is not paying attention.

Another way to avoid missing what the customer is really saying is to ask a lot of questions. If you are truly going to help your customers, there are a lot of things you need to know. Don't be afraid to ask. How can you possibly find the perfect vehicle for your customer if you don't know how they will use it, what things are important to them, what they feel they should buy, what they really want to buy and a whole lot of other pieces of information. Never assume the customer knows exactly which vehicle is correct for them. Remember, they do this once every 3 ½ or 4 years and you do this every day. If you want to build a career in this business you owe it to your customers and yourself to start paying attention to what they are and are not saying to you and begin using it to their benefit.

© VanRavenswaay 2008

Focused Selling How To: Get What You Want Through Selling

Not sure what questions to ask? Look in this month's issue for "Things I Need To Know" or ask your sales manager. Make your own list of things you feel you need to know and memorize it. When you have down time at work, spend it practicing or reviewing these questions, rather than hanging out with the coffee club at the front door. If you will start listening to your customers, you will be amazed at the results you'll get, and that is what it's all about!

Let me ask you this:

Can you see how the salesperson in this article might have gotten better results if he/she had asked more questions and paid attention to the answers?

I would have to say that you probably said yes to that question?

What do you think might have happened if the right questions were asked?

A sale?

Let me ask a different question here;

When you go into new surroundings with new people, what is the one thing you know about?

You may know absolutely nothing about where you are or the new people you are meeting, but isn't the one thing you know about... you?

Think back for a second about a time when you met somebody you didn't know. Think in particular about a time when you felt that initial meeting went exceptionally well.

What was a large part of the conversation about?

Focused Selling How To: Get What You Want Through Selling

I am willing to bet that in nine out of ten cases when an initial encounter went well for you it was because you got to talk about you or the other person showed a significant interest in knowing about you.

Have you ever heard of Dale Carnegie?

Most people have. In one of his books, he refers to the "brilliant conversationalist".

Guess what he is referring to.

He is talking about the person who enters a conversation, asks a couple of questions about the other person and then just listens.

Occasionally, he will ask an additional question to keep the information coming, but literally may only speak two or three minutes out of an hour conversation.

Why would people like this kind of person?

The truth is with the exception of very rare cases; people like to talk about themselves.

Why is this important to you in sales?

Let me ask another question.

How often do you go to work?

Well on average a salesperson works about 25 days a month so it's literally almost everyday, isn't it?

How often do people buy your product?

The average cycle for automobiles is about every 3 ½ to 4 years.

When some one comes in to buy from you; who knows more about the sales process, your products, and your business?

© VanRavenswaay 2008

Focused Selling How To: Get What You Want Through Selling

Well, unless you are brand new in sales, it is you the salesperson.

How do you think that makes the customer feel?

How would it make you feel?

When a prospect comes into your business they know that they are at a distinct disadvantage to you and it makes them extremely uncomfortable.

Have you ever had a customer say to you: "I'm just looking?"

Have you ended up selling that person your product?

It happens every day.

What's the deal?

The truth is, the prospect is uncomfortable and so they throw up defense mechanisms to slow you down.

Does that mean they aren't interested in what you're selling? Of course not, it's just their way of saying: "I'm uncomfortable, so give me my space while I try to figure things out here and level the playing field.

So what do you do to overcome this?

After I have greeted a prospect I will ask them a few different questions which will get them talking about the one thing they know about: them self.

Why would I do this?

Why would I waste my time getting them talking about themselves instead of what specifically they are looking for?

Focused Selling How To: Get What You Want Through Selling

First of all, I genuinely love people. I am fascinated by hearing their stories and who they are.

Second, I get a lot more information about how a prospect will really be using my product or services from talking about them, than I will ever get from asking only generic questions. I use a series of questions to get them started talking about themselves.

Not about me, or what kind of product they're looking for, just about them.

What have I just done for the prospect?

Didn't I just take a big step towards putting them at ease?

Didn't I also tell them, without saying a word: "This is going to be a different buying experience than what you are used to?"

Didn't I also make it much easier for me to guide them through the sales process because their perception of me is probably now that of friend versus opponent?

Yes, there are a lot of things you need to ask, but can you see how putting them at ease like this will make all of those questions much easier?

As you move further into the sales process the rapport you just built by letting them talk about themselves will be a crucial factor in the level of trust you have with the prospect.

Incidentally, if they start talking about themselves don't cut them off. Too many salespeople try to hurry this part of the process because they are uncomfortable with it. Not realizing that every other step of the process becomes easier when you build rapport.

LET THEM TALK!

When you start with questions about the individual, in other words, get them talking about themselves, you will also find that

© VanRavenswaay 2008

they will give you a lot of this information without you having to ask a specific question.

A prospect may tell you that he is a traveling salesperson and always has lots of sample cases with him that never quite to fit in his trunk. He is telling you that cargo capacity, possibly the kind you find in a wagon is really what he needs. Of course you would have to ask additional questions before making that assumption, but that is an example where he volunteered some information without being specifically asked about it?

What you will also find is that good questions generally lead to more questions. Any time you ask a question and get a response from the prospect you need to make certain that you understand the answer. This can be accomplished in a couple of ways. First you can simply repeat back to them what they have said as you understand it. In its simplest form it looks something like this:

Prospect: I really prefer something with a leather interior.

You: So you want leather interior.

This is an over simplification of the concept, but can you see how there is no confusion between the salesperson and the prospect? You as a salesperson are simply repeating what you understand the prospect said to you.

Why would you do this? Well let's look at our example to see what could happen. Our prospect said they preferred leather and we repeated that statement back to them thinking we understood.

In response to our statement the prospect takes a different turn:

You: So you want leather interior.

Prospect: Well, no. I prefer leather, but I always have kids in the car and they are always complaining about how hot the seats are. I prefer leather, but I really need something with cloth.

Focused Selling How To: Get What You Want Through Selling

Can you see why it is so very important to make certain you understand what the prospect is saying?

If you were the salesperson in the example above, what might have happened if you hadn't clarified the prospects statement?

Couldn't you have stood a good chance of losing a possible sale? Maybe you don't have a cloth option available in a vehicle that meets the rest of the prospects criteria.

Maybe the prospect would take leather interior if you focus on solutions to the seat temperature, but how could you do that if you don't know it's an issue?

If you know it could be an issue are you going to focus on the benefits of leather or are you more likely to share all of the other benefits that the vehicle offers and just spend a small amount of time on a solution to the leather problem?

Can you see the benefit to you of repeating what the prospect says to you?

The other thing you can do is to ask clarifying questions. Here is an example:

Prospect: I want something with performance.

You: What does performance mean to you?

Over the years I have found that something like performance means different things to different people. To some people it means acceleration. To others it means freeway-passing power. To others it means handling and cornering ability. If you assume that the prospect means what you perceive as performance there is a good chance you will miss it completely.

If your prospect is thinking about handling and cornering and you spend all of your time focusing on acceleration, what's going to happen?

Isn't the prospect going to think something like: "This guy doesn't really care at all about what I'm interested in?"

Isn't that a strong possibility?

Can you see why it is so important to ask clarifying questions?

Throughout this section I have talked about interpretations. In other words: words or phrases meaning different things to different people.

As a professional you also need to be very aware of the feeling certain words create in peoples minds. As I said at the beginning of our discussion about the initial contact you want to set a tone, which is emotionally positive and warm.

There are certain words you can use that will help you and there are words that will hinder you. Take a look at the two groups of words that follow to understand what I mean.

Choosing the Right Words

UNDERSTAND PROVEN HEALTH EASY GUARANTEE MONEY SAFETY SAVE NEW LOVE DISCOVERY RIGHT RESULTS TRUTH COMFORT PROUD PROFIT DESERVE HAPPY TRUST VALUE FUN VITAL INVESTMENT YOU SECURITY ADVANTAGE POSITIVE BENEFITS

DEAL COST PAY CONTRACT SIGN TRY WORRY LOSS LOSE HURT BUY DEATH BAD SELL SOLD PRICE DECISION HARD DIFFICULT OBLIGATION LIABLE FAIL LIABILITY FAILURE PAYMENT

Focused Selling How To: Get What You Want Through Selling

Although these are by no means all inclusive lists, the two groups above represent words that sell and words that un-sell.

If you look at the top group of words, as you read them you will find that in most cases they invoke positive feelings in your mind.

The bottom list in contrast, tends to invoke negative pictures in your mind.

What other words can you think of that either have a positive or negative picture attached to them specifically related to what you sell?

If you are paying attention to the prospects responses, both verbal and visual you will notice that dependant on your selection of words you can either draw them into the conversation or shut them down.

Your choice of words can go a long way towards keeping the prospect involved in the process and moving in the right direction.

In other words, it is much easier to get a customer to O.K. an agreement, than it is to get them to sign the contract.

And while we're speaking of words you use;

I don't care how you speak when you're communicating with your friends, however, when you are speaking to a prospective customer, you need to practice courtesy and respect.

There is nothing more disgusting to me than to have a salesperson talking to me in slang language, cursing and joking like I was one of his/her buddies.

As you're customer, even if I was referred to you, I expect to be treated with respect and that my friend means toning in your language.

Focused Selling How To: Get What You Want Through Selling

If you already speak courteously, with lots of; please and thank you and "Yes, sir" and Yes, Ma'am", then just keep doing what you're doing. If you don't; take a crash course on etiquette or risk turning off a lot of customers.

On a similar note, there is something else you need to be aware of.

Now I know at this point you may be thinking: "Something else to remember?"

But don't panic.

Anything worth doing in life takes time and effort. You can't possibly expect to implement everything we have and will talk about with the very next prospect you come in contact with.

It takes practice to get it right, but the more you practice and utilize all of the tools we give you here the more effective you will become.

We all know that people communicate in different manners, such as verbal, body-language to name a couple, but did you also know that we perceive our world in different manners.

Over the years a lot of research has been done in this field. It is know as Neuro-Linguistics or quite simply: brain language. We are not going to spend a tremendous amount of time on this topic, but it is an area you should be aware of as a professional salesperson.

If you would like to learn more about this topic I would recommend that you pick up one of Anthony Robbins books as he discusses it in almost all of his material.

For the moment what you really need to understand is that people perceive their world in one of three primary ways. They are listed here below:

AUDITORY

VISUAL

KINISTHETIC

Quite simply, auditory people perceive their world through sounds; visual people perceive their world through sight and kinesthetic people perceive their world through feel.

Why is this important to you as a salesperson?

They have found that a majority of males are visual. Big surprise! Let's say that you are not visual, you are auditory.

Incidentally, they have found that whatever type of person you are is how you generally communicate to others.

In other words, if you are auditory you may say things like: "I hear what you are saying."

If I am visual and you are auditory and you keep saying things like: "Do you hear what I'm saying?" or 'How does that sound to you?" what's going to happen to my interest in what you are talking about?

That's right; it's going to diminish greatly.

Fortunately, it is fairly easy to notice the different types and many people are a combination of more than one so if you don't pick up on someone's primary type you may not altogether lose them.

Focused Selling How To: Get What You Want Through Selling

How do you recognize a particular type of individual?

Let's look briefly at each of the types and give you some clues you can follow. Understand first of all that for each type there are senses that they represent.

In other words, auditory involves things you hear. Visual is obviously things you see and kinesthetic involves things you feel. With that in mind, you will find that there are certain words that the different types use often to describe their world. Here are a few examples for each type.

Auditory – hear, sound, listen, volume, loud, quiet, clear as a bell

Visual – see, sight, bright, dark, shiny, crystal clear

Kinesthetic – feel, felt, found, touch, hot, cold

What you may also find is that each of these types will act certain way when communicating with you. An auditory person for example may lean in towards you when you are speaking because sound is very important to them. A visual person may step back to get a better look at things. A kinesthetic person may put their hand on your shoulder or may touch a leather seat because that is their world.

Is this the single most important key to your success in selling?

Absolutely not, but it is another tool for your toolbox and it is certainly something worth looking at if you feel there is something you are hearing correctly from your prospect and you're just not connecting.

Above all else, when it comes to getting to know your prospect, be sincere. As the chapter title says; it's not all about you!

Will it absolutely kill you to spend a little time getting to know a fellow human being?

© VanRavenswaay 2008

Focused Selling How To: Get What You Want Through Selling

Depending on how your sales department is set up you may legitimately have to go to your sales manager to get a price quote for your product. I've seen cases where it takes all of two minutes to accomplish this and others where it can take a half an hour to get a quote.

If you're in the latter situation, don't leave your customer sitting by them self for that entire duration.

First of all it's rude. Second it gives an appearance of non-professionalism and third, that time would be much better spent talking to your customer and building even more rapport.

As long as we're on the "Don't" list here's a few more:

Don't –

- Smoke in front of your customer, even if they are smoking.

- Wear sunglasses so they can't see your eyes.

- Answer your phone for any reason while with a customer. How important do you think you make your customer feel if you are answering phone calls while working with them?

- Do anything that would generally give the impression that the customer is not the most important thing going on for you in this moment.

People can sense sincerity as sure as I'm writing these words and if you lack it; they'll know it and you probably won't be doing business with them.

Yes, in the beginning of this book I referred to focused-selling as being focused on what you want to drive your career, but in this case it's all about being focused on your customer and their wants, needs and desires.

Find that focus and you will find great success in selling.

Your Success Machine!

What do you think is the difference between having a good career and a great career?

What do the absolute best in selling do that the rest don't?

What keeps some selling while others hit dry patches on the road of life?

When I started out selling it was a different time and place. There was a time when a salesperson could show up at work and count on his/her employer to provide enough people walking through the front door to make a decent living.

What changed? What happened to those good old days when I could show up at work and have four or five people to talk to each day?

Let's look;

How many different brands and versions of the products or services you sell are available in the United States right now?

How far away is the next competitor of any brand to yours?

Where do about 80 percent of all buyers do their research today before they ever head to your business?

The answers to these questions will help you to understand what changed. The good news is once you understand today's marketplace and more specifically who your customer is; you can create your own stream of customers.

Focused Selling How To: Get What You Want Through Selling

Probably, five years ago, I heard a number somewhere around 354 different models of vehicles available for sale in the North American market. It's probably higher today. If you're in the car business, how many do you offer? Can you see how that might add a little competition to the mix?

When I started selling in my hometown back in Michigan, the next closest dealer of the same brand was 30 miles away.

Thirty miles may not seem that far today, but that was a big outing back in the early 80's. Thirty miles was a pack up the kids we're going for a drive, kind of ordeal.

Today according to research, nearly 80 percent of all new car buyers visit the internet to do research prior to even going down to the dealership.

What are the odds they might find your competition on the internet even if they live 2 blocks from your dealership?

Today, even if your product is a better fit for their needs, another manufacturer might have a better marketing plan. A plan that attracts your customers to a different brand just because of the way it appeals to their heartstrings. All over the internet before they even drive the two blocks to your business.

And if your competitor is a mega-business, which many are today, they might be spending more dollars to advertise to your customers than you are.

Economies of scale, which means the bigger you are and the more you can spend the cheaper it becomes, allows mega-groups to spend less in your neighborhood and get more benefit than you can.

They get better prices on advertising, better prices on supplies, and better deals on benefits; all of which means it's harder to compete for the "little" guy.

That being said; how can you compete and create a great career for yourself?

How can you have people lined up to see you in a marketplace with as much competition as there is today?

To do this we need to look at the key ingredients of your own personal "Success Machine".

Together we are going to turn you from a survivor into an amazing income generating machine.

You would like that wouldn't you?

You'd like to have people walking in the door asking for you, wouldn't you?

Wouldn't it be great to go home each exhausted and yet, supercharged because you were so busy you could hardly catch your breath?

That's what you can have if you learn the secrets of creating your own personal marketing machine!

Think of it as "You, Inc."

Your own personal brand that attracts people to you!

So now, let's get started on building your personal "Success Machine".

To start out building a marketing/prospecting machine that works for you, it's important to know who your customers are. I know this may come as a shock, but your product is not for everyone.

Let me repeat that; your product is not for everyone!

Focused Selling How To: Get What You Want Through Selling

The place most sales and marketing people get into trouble is in nailing down who their real target customer should be.

I will also say this in contrast; there are a lot of folks out there who are right for your product and just don't know it!

Manufacturers spend hundreds of thousands of dollars to determine who their target demographics for their products are. This is a great resource for you to use to begin to understand what types of people will be right for which product that you sell. They are not the end all, be all answer though.

You probably have product training materials in your business that relays information like; average age, average income, marital status, etc. for each of the products you represent. In the sales process this can be very useful in determining which product will be best matched, in general, to your customer.

With so much general information you have an idea who will walk in to the business to buy what product or service, but we're not really talking about the people who might consider your product in spite of you.

We're talking about the people who consider and buy your product because of you.

As we explored in the focused selling process, It's about the relationships you build. Remember;

> **"If people like you they'll listen to you. If they trust you, they'll buy from you!"**
>
> **Zig Ziglar**

Focused Selling How To: Get What You Want Through Selling

This is truly where your marketing comes from as well. Understanding how to get people to trust you just from your marketing is one of the greatest keys to success in selling.

And knowing how to market to the right people is something that will set you apart from the crowd.

Most of us are familiar with the Guinness Book of World Records. It's amazing some of the items you will find in that book. Would you believe there is actually a record for the greatest retail automotive salesman? Well, there is! His name is Joe Girard. If you ever want get your juices soaring with ideas, read his book. They're all available at { HYPERLINK "http://www.joegirard.com" }.

Joe tells in the book how he would go to sporting events with brown sacks full of business cards. When the team would score and everyone was throwing confetti, he would be tossing business cards into the air. In the early days, in that venue it was actually pretty effective. He would get people calling him or stopping by to see him at the dealership.

Incidentally, Joe holds the record because he sold incredible numbers of cars, to one customer at a time, not fleet accounts.

One by one by one! Very impressive!

Some of what Joe did back then will not work today! The whole idea here is that rather than sit around and wait, Joe went out and dreamed up new ideas to bring business to him. And it worked!

I don't want you throwing out business cards at sporting events, simply because I think we can come up with more targeted ways to reach the people you want to at very low or no cost to you. If you insist on throwing cards at sporting events, OK a long as you understand the return on investment will be low and you might get sited for littering and it is only one small part of your Success Machine!

Focused Selling How To: Get What You Want Through Selling

At any rate, those types of things are a broad blanket approach to marketing and let's be honest, you and I probably can't afford to spend the millions of dollars it would take to spread the word about us that a McDonald's or Coca-Cola can.

That's why we're going to take a more targeted approach to building your Success Machine. You may not have the resources to be the ultimate everything to everybody; you can however be the "Best of the Best", within a specific niche of prospective customers.

That's what we're going to work on here. Not world domination, just owning your own little piece of the pie.

Build the machine

Ever watch somebody at a bar or club or a sporting event or even at church who is obviously looking for a date?

They walk in not sure what they're looking for and start to interact with people or maybe just watch from the sidelines. The room is full of potential dates and yet they can leave without even having a good prospect for the future. Maybe they even leave so frustrated that they decide they're never going to find that special someone, so they might as well give up.

What happens?

Why don't they find their future mate in that moment?

What could they do differently?

We're talking about looking for potential customers here, but the two are not that different. Chances are good they don't have a clear image in their mind of what kind of mate they are really seeking and they're hoping something will catch their eye.

Wow! Kind of a scary proposition don't you think?

Focused Selling How To: Get What You Want Through Selling

So what's so different about that and looking for customers that way?

Absolutely nothing!

The first step in building the machine is to decide what you're looking for in a customer.

Who are they?

Where are they?

What problems do they have which you and your product can solve?

Where do they shop?

Where do they live?

What kind of activities do they participate in?

Are they married or single or does it even matter?

What associations are they a part of?

Do they network themselves?

Can you develop a mutual relationship based on referrals?

Where do they dine?

What do you have in common with them?

Who do you know that they know?

When you can answer these or at least some of these questions you will begin to have an idea who it is, you are after and where to find them and how to reach them. Before we get into who they are, let's get into who you are. A machine that just runs people down doesn't do you or me any good. A machine that carries a pleasant message that's scratches where they have itches will attract them like bees to honey.

Let's create a message that will be so sweet to the ears of those who you specifically target they won't be able to resist it.

Who are you?

If you want to attract people you have to summarize yourself in a way they will be able to understand.

You need to develop your "elevator" speech.

You know the one where you have maybe two floors on an elevator with someone in order to at least peak their curiosity for more. You meet a beautiful lady on the elevator; you have to say something that will get her attention with out getting you slapped, if you want any chance of making a future connection. This is the same sort of message.

The answers you provide below will help us create that message. Remember one thing though, you will not attract every one you come in contact with and everyone you come in contact with will not be right for you to market to.

Answer these questions honestly and you will be able to create a powerful message to attract your preferred customer.

1. What are your values in life?

_____

_____

_____

Focused Selling How To: Get What You Want Through Selling

OK, so this was not the question you expected right out of the gate!

But, let's look at this!

What's most important to you as we have discussed through Focused Selling, determines what you do every day and how satisfied with each and every moment you live.

Not clearly knowing what you value or what's most important to you will cause you to be inconsistent in the moments when you most need to be who you are.

Your ability to be a trustworthy person in others' eyes is directly affected by you knowing who you are.

I'll give you a formula for determining your values and then I'll even give you my list of values as an example. You have got to start here in order to hone in on your true 30 second speech to prospective customers.

Believe me when I say; what you sell is not nearly as important as the man/woman selling it!

To easily determine your values ask yourself the following questions about the different areas of your life:

What's most important to you in the area of relationships (health, finances, family, etc.) in your life?

What must happen for you to know you have it?

How will you be when you have this in your life?

Is this something you must have, do or be; or is it just something you'd like to have? If it's not a must, it's probably not a value.

You can ask these simple questions about every area of your life and in the end, if you are really honest, you will have a list of values and what they mean to you like this list below.

My Values –

INTEGRITY
The highest irreproachable level of pure honest congruent being.

PASSION
Driven by unrelenting levels of enthusiasm.

HEALTH & VITALITY
A high level of physical and emotional well-being which not only affords undiluted passion today, but continually builds reserves for tomorrow.

LOVE
A feeling of unconditional caring.

COMPASSION
A deep seeded concern for the well-being of others, A driving force for servitude and contribution.

ADVENTURE
A driving sense of seeking the exciting with a "Why Not?" attitude.

JOY
An overwhelming combination of happiness and peace.

GRATITUDE
An understanding that life is a gift from God not to be taken for granted.

FEARLESSNESS
Having the ability to act without the normal restraints of hesitation and over analysis.

Focused Selling How To: Get What You Want Through Selling

DYNAMIC
Having a charisma that emanates my personal sense without the need for words.

EMPOWERING
Being able to help others reach new levels of self-belief.

EMPATHETIC
Being able to hear and understand and feel others problems without becoming the problems.

SPIRITUAL
To view life as if through the eyes of God or from His perspective.

CREATIVE
If you look hard enough there is an answer to every question.

INQUISITIVE
Having the drive to ask all of the questions in order to understand, help and improve.

PROVOCATIVE
Never settling for the "easy" answer when the truth is one painful question away.

POWERFUL
A feeling that drives everything physical, emotional and spiritual.

FLEXIBLE
Having the ability to "bend" my path without "breaking" my goals.

SECURITY
Having the financial strength to support and enhance my contribution goals and focus.

Focused Selling How To: Get What You Want Through Selling

Values are not things you would like to have in your life. They are those things you absolutely can not live without in your life. They are the things that in order for you to feel completely congruent on a regular daily basis they must be met.

Ever go through a day where everything on your list got accomplished and yet still you felt empty inside?

There's a pretty good chance you did a lot of the stuff on your list outside of your values. You might have even done things you felt were wrong just to get them done and out of the way. It happens to all of us at some time, but if it's a regular occurrence in your life, you are setting your self up to be miserable.

You can't live; day in and day out, at odds with your values and be completely happy in life!

If you are telling people one thing about yourself and living a different way they will pick up on that so fast it will make your head spin. More importantly, they will not trust you as far as they can throw you!

Have you ever had a conversation with someone you felt was really just telling you what you wanted to hear?

Sure you have!

We have all had that kind of conversation at one point or another.

How did that conversation make you feel?

Did you feel like the entire time you were speaking, they were just waiting for their turn to talk or maybe they even kept cutting you off so they could make their point?

What did you think about that person?

© VanRavenswaay 2008

Did it bother you enough that you mentioned it to others?

That's the kind of PR you don't want for your self. Take the time right now to figure out your values and get clear about them. You'll thank yourself later for doing this, trust me.

OK, so now that we got that handled, let's go back to writing your 30 second speeches.

2. What is unique about what you do for your customers?

_____

_____

_____

_____

3. Why should someone buy from you versus your competition?

_____

_____

4. What are some of the problems that you solve for your customers?

_____

_____

_____

_____

Here's an interesting bit of info; the results of a recent online survey I conducted showed that although most people have some unique desires for their life, there are three things that everyone mentions as ultimately important in their life.

First, is a need to feel loved. By family, by society, by significant others.

© VanRavenswaay 2008

Focused Selling How To: Get What You Want Through Selling

Second, was a need for financial security. Not a need to be rich, but to have financial stability.

And third, was a need for more time to do what they want to do in life. Whether that be to go on vacation or to work on personal goals or to spend more quality time with family and friends.

My challenge to you now is to take what you have listed above as your attributes and match them to what people say is most important to them.

In other words, how does what you do scratch where they itch? An example might be something like this;

I represent the Volvo family of vehicles. Our reputation for durability as well as our great family of fuel efficient cars will keep your money where you want it… in your pocket.

Or;

I do all of the leg work for my customers so they can spend their time where they really want to… with their family and friends.

Do you get the idea?

What do you do that meets the needs and desires of your customers while allowing you to be congruent with whom you are?

Don't promise people you offer a service if it would be a complete violation of your values.

Take your time and work on this. You may come up with something you like right away, or you may have to walk away from this exercise for a day or two.

Just keep at it until you come up with one or two sentences that really fit you.

Who Do You Want To Sell To?

At your place of business, you really don't get to choose who you want to work with. You will end up dealing with whoever walks through the door. So if you are going to create a machine to market to people, why not market specifically to those people who are congruent with your values?

Now that you know who you are and what you have to offer to your customers that will meet their needs and desires, let's figure out who your customers really are.

Answer these questions below to start to formulate your Success Machine fuel:

1. What types of activities do your ideal customers like to take part in?

2. Where do your customers shop?

3. Where do you customers live?

4. How much money do they make?

5. What websites do they visit?

6. What blog sites do they visit?

7. What type of work do your customers do?

8. What types of vehicles do they drive?

9. Do they have political affiliations?

10. What associations do they belong to?

Take some time to answer these questions. You may not know the answers to all of these questions, but I'll bet you can find them by doing a little research on the internet or simply by giving them a simple questionnaire to fill out.

Interview them. Get a group of people you feel fit this profile and buy them a cup of coffee if they will let you interview them.

Take as much time as you need to get this right, because it is crucial to creating a true marketing machine.

Let's Build The Machine

Once you have the answers to the questions I've just asked you, it's time to build the machine.

The reason I had you spend so much time on you and who you want to deal with is simple math. Unless you're made of money, there is a limit to how much you can spend when it comes to creating your own source of prospects and ultimately customers.

The more closely you match yourself and the people you want to deal with, the closer you're prospects are to being customers when you meet them for the very first time.

If you have found where your customers are, and you know that you can scratch where they itch, you are going to have a machine that will truly work for you.

There are several low cost or no cost things you can do to meet your prospects where they are. Here are a few:

1. Join the associations your potential prospects are members of. Most associations have some type of membership mixer for the purpose of bring their members together to network. Don't force yourself on people, just be an active member. Once people see that you are sincere, they will naturally seek you out.

2. Visit the same blog sites. Join the chat rooms where they are and get involved in the conversations. People are naturally drawn to others who contribute to worthwhile conversations whether in person or on the web.

3. Write your own blog on the web. You can get one for free at Blogger.com. If your blog is interesting to the people you want to do business with they will read it regularly and probably tell others they know who are also a match for you about the blog.

4. Write articles for free for the sites they visit. People look at authors as experts and trust is built quickly.

5. Do business with them. People like to deal with people who reciprocate. Obviously, if your prospect sells jetliners, you may not be a valid prospect for them, but if your target prospects are local store or business owners you can frequent there establishments.

A word of caution, don't just become a visitor waiting for the right time to spring your self on them. Be a customer.

6. Go door to door to neighborhood businesses introducing yourself. Most small business owners can buy your product. Don't expect overnight business and don't be pushy. A cordial introduction is all that is required to let them know who you are and will go much further than an interrogation.

7. Gather email addresses everywhere you go. Make certain that you get permission to send updates every so often regarding your business. Do not add someone to your email list without their permission. It's the fastest way to get your self blackballed with a group of people. If asked most people will be more than happy to let you

send them something every now and again, but if you do it without permission, that's something else.

8. Create an easy e-Newsletter which you can send out on a quarterly basis. Many companies send monthly, even weekly newsletters, but they sooner or later end up in my "junk-mail" or "blocked-sender" folder. Make sure the newsletter is full of real information and news.

People will soon opt-out of newsletters if they are perceived as nothing more than an advertisement.

9. Schedule quarterly phone follow-up with your current customers. They are your best source of new customers. Keep yourself front of mind with these folks and you will have people lined up outside your office waiting to get in to buy. You can purchase expensive sets of cards you can mail regularly, just because. Keep yourself in their mind at all times. And never, ever, ever avoid them if they come in to your place of business with a problem. Instead be right there helping them get service right away.

10. All of these items are easily kept running using a program like Microsoft Outlook. You can schedule all of your calls and cards and emails in one convenient place. Your business may also have a CRM (Customer Relationship Management) system which will do all of the same things for you. Check with your manager for details. I've never heard a manager say, don't follow-up or prospect to a sales person.

11. For a few dollars a month you can probably run a business card size ad in your local paper. If done consistently, it will have an impact, because most people just want a name they are familiar with when they go to business.

12. Attend every event you can for your local Chamber of Commerce. The members are business people, most of whom can afford to buy your product.

Build, build, and build. Don't stop and soon enough you'll have more people wanting to do business with you than you can get to in a day.

One more thing;

Be a real person. Honest-sincere-friendly-caring-outgoing. Be all of these things and do it without being prompted.

People can tell a sincere person from a mile away. They can also tell fake from farther than that.

Be sincere and watch your Success Machine grow and grow.

Gratitude

If you truly want more of what life has to offer there is one other item we have to address before we're done.

As I have discussed several times throughout this book, selling is a highly emotional business. It can be as inspiring as any other and it can also be extremely tasking.

There may be days when you just don't feel like getting out there and selling.

What you do in those times is what will determine what you do in the good times as well. There are things you can do on a daily basis that will guarantee that you will have more up days than down.

First, is to learn to practice gratitude.

You may be thinking; I don't have anything to be grateful for!

The more you show gratitude for the things you already have, the more you will have to show gratitude for!

Zig Ziglar

Not to over simplify things, but can you read these words?

If you can you have a gift that many in this world would do anything to have.

Don't get me wrong. I'm not talking about the kind of gratitude you were taught when you were a kid. You know the manners; "Please" and "Thank You". Most of us were taught to always say thank you as a child.

As an adult, it becomes so much of an automated response that not only do we not realize we're saying it; we don't get any of the emotional connection that true gratitude brings about.

So, what am I talking about here?

I had a heart attack this year. Do you think that the fact that I am able to write these words might be cause for a little gratitude?

You better believe it.

But, it's much more than just that. Every day when I wake up I express gratitude for the fact that I have the opportunity once again to choose whatever life I want to live.

As I write these words, I am having some issues with my laptop computer. It would be easy to get upset and whiny about the fact that this stupid computer is on the fritz.

Let me ask you this; what exactly would that change?

Would my computer start working better because I spent my emotional energy complaining about it?

Yeah, I don't think so!

The truth is I am writing these words on a computer. Something we all take for granted because we have them. Do you think that there might be someone out there in this world who would love to have this laptop no matter how many times they had to reboot it?

This is not about feeling sorry for someone else, its about appreciating what we have. If I am positively focused on how great it is to have a computer to work on, that's what I'm going to get more of.

If I focus on how bad this computer is working, guess what I'm going to get more of? Where's my focus going to be all day long if I keep complaining about my computer?

What kind of day is that going to produce for me?

As I sit here writing about gratitude, I can't help but take a couple of minutes in the middle of the day and reflect on all of the things I have to be grateful for in my life both in the present and in the future.

Yes, the future!

If you are truly grateful for the things you already have in life, why wouldn't you expect that more good things are coming your way in the near future?

That's what gratitude does for you. It sets a level of expectation for your life.

How can you use this in the sales environment?

Let's say you have a situation with a customer that is less than perfect. You end up spending lots of time and eventually end up with no sale.

What's the typical response to a situation like that?

Don't we get upset at the customer? Call them a jerk? Accuse them of wasting our time?

Obviously, investing a lot of time into a relationship with a customer and not making a sale is not the ideal situation for any of us, but let's look at how you can turn this around into something positive.

What are you grateful about in this particular case?

And you of course respond with; Nothing!

What could you be grateful for in this situation if you really looked at it?

Did you learn something about yourself? Did you learn something about your product? Maybe this was not really someone you want in the long term as a customer anyway.

Let me ask you this;

If you stay in a place of upset, what are you going to be like for the next customer you deal with?

What are your chances of getting the customer who walked out back and turning things around if you are sitting there all upset and whiny?

What's the rest of your day going to be like if you can't be grateful for the opportunity and move past it?

Want some things to be grateful for?

If you have a job in sales, you have employment, an opportunity, probably an office (even if it's shared), a phone, probably internet/email access, a decent product, somebody else to pay the utilities, pay for the advertising, pay for the inventory. You likely have health insurance, maybe a 401k plan, and very likely at least a few great co-workers to support your efforts.

That's an awful lot to be grateful for if you ask me. In addition to that, if you're even half way decent as a salesperson, if you not happy with your current company, you can go get another job.

Whether the economy is good or bad, companies don't usually eliminate sales positions. At least not the true commission kind.

Focused Selling How To: Get What You Want Through Selling

If you want to completely change industries as a salesperson you have the distinct advantage of knowing how to sell your self.

There are loads of things to be grateful for and when you start to show that gratitude, more great things begin to show up in your life.

If you are a truly grateful person, every time you meet a new prospective customer you will be grateful for the opportunity and that feeling is transferred to them. It's the way you smile or show your appreciation that creates more opportunities for gratitude.

I can and probably should, no probably will write an entire book on gratitude because it has had such a huge impact in my life.

Here's my quick formula for maintaining a life of gratitude:

1. At least once a day, personally I recommend first thing in the morning and last thing at night, take time to think about the things you are grateful for right now in your life.

2. When you encounter a situation which is less than what you'd hoped for, acknowledge that although it may not be exactly what you wanted, there are still certain aspects for which you can be grateful. Doing this will allow you to move past the negative emotions you are carrying with you about this situation.

3. Express gratitude for those things that are coming into your future. Note: If you can show gratitude for them as though they are already in your life, that's even better!

Learning to express gratitude will make you a better all around human being and a far superior salesperson as well.

Remember as we wrap up here that Focused Selling is about knowing what you want, knowing who you are, getting to know your customer, choosing who to work with and being grateful for all that life has given to you now and in the future.

Happy Selling!

Tim VanRavenswaay

Appendix

Suggested Reading
Zig Ziglar's Secrets Of Closing The Sale *by Zig Ziglar*

Ziglar On Selling *by Zig Ziglar*

Sales prospecting For DUMMIES *by Tom Hopkins*

How To Master The Art Of Selling *by Tom Hopkins*

How To Win Friends and Influence People *by Dale Carnegie*

The Power Of Positive Thinking *by Dr. Norman Vincent Peale*

How I Multiplied My Income and Increased My Happiness In Selling *by Frank Bettger*

How To Sell Anything To Anybody *by Joe Girard*

How I Raised Myself From Failure To Success In Selling *by Frank Bettger*

See You At The Top *by Zig Ziglar*

Focused Selling How To: Get What You Want Through
Selling

Over The Top *by Zig Ziglar*

A View From The Top *by Zig Ziglar*

Awaken The Giant Within *by Anthony Robbins*

The Attractor Factor *by Joe Vitale*

Harmonic Wealth *by James Arthur Ray*

The Science of Getting Rich *by Wallace D. Wattles*

Think and Grow Rich *by Napolean Hill*

Want more tips on Focused Selling? Check out Tim's Blog at:

http://focusedselling.blogspot.com